White Moth

Poetry by Maya Elphick

Printed in the United States of America

First Printing, 2019

ISBN 978-1-949321-11-1

All writings within this book belong to the author.

Cover Art Image by: Fahmida Abu Talha

A.B.Baird Publishing
66548 Highway 203
La Grande OR, 97850
USA

www.abbairdpublishing.com

Table of contents

Table of Contents Continued

Table of Contents Continued

Table of Contents Continued

Acknowledgements

I must first thank my publisher, Austie M. Baird, for her faith in my poetry and the publishing opportunities she has given me in her anthologies, thus providing great exposure for my work. I would also like to thank her for being so patient with me throughout this process and ensuring that we created exactly the right feel for this book. I must too thank Nic Outterside, Esther Morgan and Elaine Faye who each took the time to give me their invaluable feedback on the first draft of my manuscript. I am so grateful to you all for reassuring me with your experience, knowledge and creativity. I'd like to thank Fahmida, a fellow poet, for creating such wonderful artwork for this book in such a collaborative and thoughtful way. I must finally thank my family for being so wildly encouraging and supportive over the years.

For my parents, my first poets.

Square One

and I'm here again
always here again
washing my bedsheets
and wishing your words
had never fallen where they did
right by my bed
right by my head
and in the mattress too
stamping love into the carpet
in combat boots
pulling the stitches
from my night dress
using the thread
for your own uses
and leaving me
naked
and cold
and open to you
again

Moors

There is something distraught here
among the hills blushed with forest,
the hint of rebirth in the crop,
a gentle push in the stomach,
a weight planted deep in the gut.
Left like a loner in the green,
clawing up at the clouds in clean strokes,
pulling the grey down
and casting shadows on the brick.
I see no beauty
just sharp edges
and teeth glinting from basalt ridges.
I could be lost here forever
under the arm of an oak tree or
standing stark in the middle
of the cobbled street.
You would not find me,
faceless in the space between,
a hard, jagged future.
There is
a violence,
a ruthlessness in its nature.

The Passing

one day
I will wake up to a world that no longer needs me
my feet will crack as they hit the floor
and my hands will peel away
into pages of diary entries
left on the pillows of those I love most
and my children will cry soft
as the morning shines on my paper body

I think I will cry
because I will never be ready to leave
or slip into the darkness with her
even when my mother's hands reach out
to tuck a curl behind my ear
I will fear the new days of living
but I will feign bravery
as I am lifted
a cold thing in the dirt
a portrait painted by a stranger

I may leave my eyes
ears and mouth behind
tucked underneath the arms of trees
I will show off my empty face
and rest in my father's palm
as he recites stories
I have heard but will not hear again

this is where I will go
even when I don't
even when my body sinks into the ground
and my name is swallowed by generations
this is where I will be
still counting stars
still dreaming of an afterlife

Sleep Eight Hours

I found a man
who knew the land
and knew the names
of Renaissance paintings.
He lived late
so I shifted my evenings back,
made my dinners black,
bedtime at 2am pitch.
He dragged the bed over to the balcony
to fall asleep under stars,
under streetlights.
We felt rich
for the night
like runaways,
like the cat in the ally
sat on the highest step of the fire escape.

Beaches

I'm waiting for something to move me,
fall through me
like rain hitting sand,
or your thumb on my hand

> back
> and
> forth
>   soft
>   then
>   rough

until the clock stops all together
and words don't flow through my lips,
and love doesn't pour from my hips,
still waiting for something to move me,
fall through me
like rain hitting sand.

Table Manners

they say we're unstable
trying to eat off wobbly tables
too much sugar in our diets
and socially smoking every night
I'm still on Prozac
you're still on something else
blindly but kindly
spending our evenings
trying not to bite the spoon

Uproot

I must leave now. I must somehow
unstitch myself from the ground
like a silver birch. Tall, pale body
tugging its roots from the earth,

giving birth to a new life on
the other side of the river.
Pin me down like Gulliver.
Pull me back like a child

wandering too close to the edge
of the crumbling cliff face.
Give me reasons to stay.
Let storm blow my leaves away,

leave me devastated and bare.
An old boney hand reaching out
from the mud. She wants her heirlooms
back. Skin and bone react

to make soil, a powder from which
I rise, boil in the heat.
Let me wither in this state,
I do not believe in this thing you call fate.

Endless

rip my lip
with precision
let the words
break the silence
like a knife cutting through water
I love
don't love
you anymore
I'm sorry
but all things end
> ~ except heartbreak of course

Hostage

Maybe I want to live in a kind place
where people don't leave
because they'd miss your smile too much.
I want to breathe the air
the trees have made
in a place where they stand taller than money
and leaves don't shed in autumn.
I want to dance in a home with music
where your fingerprints stain the wallpaper
and the carpet holds me like a child.
Maybe I want to live in a tender place
where you sit beside me because you love me
and not because you're glued there.

Blackout

we choose to see him under moonlight
not white strip lights
stuck to the ceiling and flickering
now and again
and when they finally go out
it all seems so clear
because our hands are empty
and his footsteps are quiet
and he's already left before we can find the switch
he was waiting for this opportunity
and he ran with it
ran so far he's just a dot on our heart's horizon
or a speck of dust in our eye
that we blink out
and wipe away

The Family Tree

my women
my ancestors
lay lungs and legs before me
breathe and run
touch the sun with an extended arm
a flat palm
let the light invade the cold black
the iris
the throat
the eyelashes that flex
with dust
like spiderweb dream catchers
sculpted bodies dance at sunset
inside my wearing muscle they rest
their strength is eternal
internal
and forever knocking on my bones
opening up doors
they shut within themselves
once upon a time
when I was just a twinkle in the eye

Reach

the sheets write scarce against my skin
and my body reaches further
and fresh like a flower
or a tower inside my stomach
breaking through scalps and ceilings
and reeling mothers
mourning for my pale complexion
fill the spaces in between with
hot tea and talking
tell me how windows frost
and hearts thaw
but don't doubt me at sunrise
when I've forgotten it all

Hotel

I still like the sound of rain
and all the other things artistic people
are supposed to like,
but I like it less than silence.
Complete quiet is preferable.
A sparse room void of attachments
to my home, or my mother or my bookcase,
and a bed that's just empty enough
for me to fit into.
Enough space for an inch of sheet
between our sweaty bodies,
and an air conditioner loud enough
to drown out the sound of your breathing.
Just a small mechanical hum,
mistaken for silence
if you listen hard enough.
And I still like the moon of course,
the danger in the night,
but I think I need sunlight today.
Just enough to bleach out your figure
from the bed frame,
leaving me alone
but satisfied
in a day that won't know me at all.

Dew

in this garden
I might be something more
a figure over a flower
a hand gripping a stem

   pluck, pluck
petals from loves and love nots
are lulled and fall into the breeze
heads rolled back and eyes sleepy

I tease the roots and plant deep
soil under my fingernails
stuck stubbornly against pink flesh
like shadows in fresh desert

My Blood

I'm on the kitchen floor again
blood cold on my cheek
hair tips tinted pink
no voice at all
he left a while ago now
but these old wounds still spit out bullets
occasionally

and you lost your baby again
smile stretched before me
in soft skin
staring at old sonograms
guided through the backdoor
of the ward
for the second time

Mum's hiding her picture frames
again
and lighting candles
compulsively
she barely looks at the TV
and the news makes us all cry

Dad lives in a hollow house
a starving, bloated belly
but fat with words he can't say
to a woman who never hears them
anyway
but he perseveres
building new rooms to scream into

we're all going through the motions
loving desperately but
never questioning
because we learnt that
nothing's fair
a long time ago

High-Rise

I won't let them hurt you.
Knives can't cut through feeling
and boy, do I have enough to build walls sky high,
walls around you and bricks by your feet,
rising
    rising
like triumphant women from the earth
and smooth bloated stomachs
forming hillside.
And as they rise,
the red soles of feet will plant into the soil
and the red brick will bleed
so you don't have to.
I won't let them hurt you,
I'll stand tall and steady
but know you can climb the walls
and face them
whenever you are ready.

Bedshaped

I burn against your blue jeans
my body flexed
stretched
on the bed
you made
ten minutes before I arrived
and I'm giving you reasons
and I apologise
for wearing lipstick so carelessly
as you knot my hair
between your fingers
and paint figures in the shag carpet
and laugh about it all
like you never cared a bit

Closer Than They Appear

I'm not sure if I hear running
or just the engine humming
but something comes.
I hear a voice,
a stranger's,
but it must be someone I know.
It's hard for the imagination to work alone,
make up that rhythm, those words, that tone
coming from the backseat,
coming to attack me
in my sleep,
watch me breathe,
chest heave beneath the seat belt.
Maybe I can dream you away.
Heavy lights shine on the dash,
on my shoes that scuff the plastic.
Breathing grows deeper, steeper and rushed
as the night bus driver
stares in through the window.
Can they see it
sat behind me,
knees pressed into my back,
chin on my shoulder?
They said when I grew older
it would leave,
but it's here
constantly
and people always forget that objects may be
closer than they appear.

A Sibyl

In the last hour of the day,
before I'm asleep
but not quite awake,
it comes to me.
Words, moments,
like prophesies from a Sibyl,
like my grandmother's childhood stories.
It floods and drowns.
It weighs the bed down.
It bubbles in my stomach like Coco-Cola.
It makes me feel older.
It makes me feel seventeen.
I write, type,
I drain it.
Swing bucketfuls out onto the page,
the splashes dry,
leaving poetry.

Rejection Letter

An unspoiled day,
a well-sung hymn,
a neat fold in a rejection letter
from you,
fully explained.
My words still
fight amongst themselves
leaving inky marks
on the paper.
They left smudges on your fingertips,
on your white linen dress,
and now you hate them,
can't read them.
Messy little shits.
Ruining my chances,
staining everything.
A black sock in a white wash.
Look at this grey face of mine
and the slack mouth
full of lies.

Cut

It was all like film
from a Super 8 camera,

moments rushing into one another
like dazed children,

pushing a million days
into one seamless motion,

but no one notices how many times
we've skinned our knees.

The Feed

I roll the worm
like a cigarette
between the long green tongs,
pinch its sides,
a body of brown rings.

His small beady eye watches.
His beard patched
with triangular scales
that ripple over his bones.
I bring the wriggling thing closer to him.

He snicks his lips,
sweeps it away into his mouth
with a flat fleshy tongue.
Crunch and swallow.
The meal is done.

I am cruel,
a host, a feeder, an insect butcherer.
No better than the child
magnifying sun beams
and sizzling ants on the concrete.

The Artefact

I know why he stopped texting.
He got a glimpse of the madness I think,
read the poetry,
watched the body move through small spaces
and smile with all four limbs.
He thinks I'm a strange thing
that crawled out from the rocks
with fossil teeth
that chatter when they get excited
and bite when they get happy.
But my old smile is inbuilt,
a gift from my grandfather
who warned me about scared boys
and sacred relics.
It takes time for them to become something.

Suit

I will follow you there
in the back of a white removal van

I'll hide, crunch up real tight
a stowaway

a mosquito bite that won't fade
I'll make my mark on you

in more than one way
pick up the strays

pull at their leashes, their ears
their tails, hear them wail

by your back door
I'll do what has not been done before

I'll make a beast of the man in the tie
and I'll drag him by it

Power Cut

Let the wax drip down from the candlestick,
tears down a child's pale face.
We live and breathe tonight
under halos of dust,
blonde hair catching in the yellow light.
The wick warps,
carrying the weight of the flame
with the grace of Ra,
slim body beading with sweat
that pools at its feet.
I narrow my eyes,
try to find the trace my pen left behind
in the dim glow of the living room.
Ink sinking through paper
and onto my jeans,
little black sheep against the blue.
I read what I have written,
so black, so black,
in this dim yellow light.

The Guest

one day I'll own a house
and paint it blue
and place ferns on the window sill
I'll watch my dog find the sunny spots on the carpet
and spy my name on the spines of books on the shelf
I'll sit pretty on my spiral staircase
pull my legs against my chest
and I'll   rest   rest   rest

Floor Plan

I love you.
  I love you
in every room,
every chamber of every bloody beating organ.
I love you ugly.
I love you raw
like a sore thumb
picking at a lock
for years,
peaking through the keyhole,
watching women in red dresses
move lightly without touching the floor.
Their feet smooth and petite
until they kick down the door
and flatten me.
I love you deep.
I love you vertical and tall,
grey like brutalist architecture,
pale like the skin I wear
and the cheeks I brush beige.
I love you in every single way
that is unfashionable.
I don't love you like a feminist
or a romance agnostic,
I love you like a gossip,
like a loud-mouthed neurotic
that bathes in the blood of bleeding ears,
sick of hearing about your blue eyes.
I love you dangerous.
I love you painful
and without purpose
like the light switch I flick five times
so the houses don't burn down
and the fire doesn't swallow
all those rooms I use
to love you

                                        secretly.

Quiver

I lay my hand on your skin and
read the goosebumps like Braille.
Watch the hairs on
the pale curve of your stomach
rise to meet me,
wisps bending like saplings
on river banks.
You shiver as
the soft pads of my fingertips
dig
and uproot.

Edits

At 1am we talk on the phone about your poetry,
dissecting lines of your handwriting
like wiry black bodies on white pages,
wriggling away from our scalpels
as we scrape the fat from their bones.
Slim enough to slip between lips
and be spoken on stages,
but as we strip them bare
the words reach out from our laps
and punch us,
knocking our pearly teeth out onto the paper
before being absorbed and stolen.
Now the anorexic bodies can bite
and they are hungry.
The verse nibbles at our fingertips,
taking back what we cut off
until our mouths can't open and shut
and our forked tongues can only hiss
as the poetry does the talking.

Nineteen

We are young,
soft-skinned babies
crying over moonlight passages on the water.
You are ankle-deep
and drunk,
waving your arms at me,
the glass brushing up against your ring,
a high note on a violin string.
You reiterate your point
until my glazed eyes focus,
stepping forward along
the white ripples on the river.
Do you see it shimmer?
That silver pavement glimmer
and stretch out into those stary spectators,
mocking our bright ambition?
You take a swig
and move onwards,
pushing out into the deep,
a warmth rising in your belly
like the whiskey in your hand.

A United State

I came here to find myself,
remind myself
of the structure.
The way the bricks meet,
the way you build walls
for lovers to press their palms against;
fists through terracotta,
scratch marks in the clay.
They will have their day,
when the old are dead and forgetful.
And I came here to learn the language my body speaks
and read the words that leak
through the pauses in your speech
about walls and about lovers that weren't meant to be.
I came here to obey your laws,
walk your flaws
and deny
smash smash smash
the wall.
I came here to watch my eyes dilate in the mirror,
from great again to pinhole small.
I came here to shoot to kill,
to fire, to blow, to hit, to blast.
I came here to understand you,
I thought you'd never ask.

One

Maybe my biggest mistake was believing
I was alone in being lonely,
when we all spend nights in bed
trying to find a pair of eyes in the artex ceiling
and laying in baths longer than necessary
to feel warmth in the evening.
I just want to go to a party
where someone looks,
lusts
then loves me.

Esther Greenwood

I don't know where it all went:
the pearlescent sheen of my mother's hair,
the smile in my sister's voice,
the tramp on the street,
the bus stop.

The bus stopped stopping for me
just leaned into the puddles by the pavement,
spat into my hair,
darkened the roots,
laughed dryly
and left my socks soaked through.

I don't know where it all went,
where the love went,
where it stopped
and found a better place.
Where it sits,
how it sits,
legs crossed or undone.
Thinking about me still?
Probably not.
Probably smoking with the windows closed.

I don't know where it all went:
the spider in the glass,
the key to my safe,
the good fight.

I don't know where she went,
sweet Sylvia,
smile dressed to the nines.
Help me find her,
maybe I'll find the rest there too.

Dentist

Smile
and like teeth
and fillings,
the world will come apart.
Bleeding gums
and melting ice,
tears making stones softer
and oceans
just a little
more
salty.

Shoplifter

I'm behind the counter,
smiling in my lanyard.
Breath sticks to the walls in hot boredom
and an endless plucking of guitar strings
bounces across the speakers
like a dripping tap.
A grainy figure shudders across the small screen,
I watch him
framed in grey, dodging the static.
He scrapes his finger across shelves of little things,
fingers move like hinges,
nails scratch like records.
He pulls something up into his sleeve,
eyes dart to the left,
checking the camera,
checking who's buying.
I think, I rub my fingers together,
I stay quiet,
I keep smiling.

Helium

She's a loved up,
pumped up,
plump pink balloon.
She will drag you forever
unless you cut the string.
Teeth sit, ivory chips between her lips,
plump pink balloons
gagging.
She trots like a horse,
shits in the road,
skips her grit all over you,
pebble-scattered pavement face
for her to walk on
in her high heeled shoes,
your punctured lung
a deflated pink balloon.
Hark, she comes.
Grin sucker, grin.
            (Cut the damn string)

Dylan

The weather dial turns to you
and your chalky cliffs.
Tiles smash against the stone,
thrown from the roof by stormy sighs,
thunderous groans.
You've lost your muse,
your inspiration.
What once whetted your lips
and floated in a bottle
has dried up,
along with the love you had for your wife.
Her red lips smeared onto her cheeks,
a faded rosiness,
a parched beauty.
And the nights are cold and
come with a dark metal taste,
a flooding of black stars,
a howl down the chimney
that wakes the baby.
You say you've lost your muse,
all torn up with the bed sheets,
cheeks
red like late leaves.
What are you now?
A hack, a loner, a thief.
A man who makes money,
spends money
on grief.

Pray

We all feel those eyes of stained glass
that fall so surely upon our backs
in loud, silent cathedrals.
They look down,
up,
confused
and so deeply disappointed
by the new light
that pours through them,
a harsh light that no longer
seems to come from the sky.
Lips press feet
and hands clasp something
that once felt so certain:
a cross,
a man,
a time saved for worship
to the one who gave us eyes
to be blind with,
one to be denied.
But no one realised we'd take it so far,
that we'd be running down the steps
because the climb took too much time
and we all have better things to do now
anyway.
But on the occasion
there's nothing much new
and we resort to the past
for a Sunday afternoon.
We'll visit your churches,
and hope you can't see through us
as clearly as we see through you.

Night Drives

service station lights
call through midnight
biting into the side of a highway
light shaping the clouds into days spent
hungry and restless
as the road hits the horizon
stretching out like Gatsby's dock
towards something greater
a new day
a turning in the distance
a new light made
for the blind
and something for
the heartless to love
at nighttime

Aflame

you hold me as if I'll snap
break like words
and fold like paper envelopes
love letters sent
licked with hope

you kiss me as if I'll melt
like glaciers
like wax faces
you're not walking on ice, you know
I am strong enough to hold you

you love me as if I'll fall
I'll slip and trip and call
for your hand
as my feet crumble into you
my arms reach out to you
but I can stand without you

because
warmth doesn't mean fire
you know

and I am strong
you know

Runaways

love writes its stories
in paper cuts
on the skin of
pink lovers
blushing and sitting between
wide teeth grinning
who don't notice the wounds
sliced and sore
until the door has been closed on them
and the playlist has ended and
the blood runs
away with
him too

Tempest

You've got that look in your eye
as if strength comes as easily as breath,
and you talk like oxygen is a light thing
the breeze could blow away.
And yet
you can barely stand up on stormy days,
too heavy
in those thundercloud boots
you wear.

So we all keep quiet
and silence the storm,
tongues
taped
to the roofs
of our mouths,
stopping the words coming out
and showing you only the kind ones
that apologise
for the weather and try to change it for you,
no matter how many times your
lightening strikes down our houses.

Into The Deep Dark Wood

He's like my boyfriend
but worse.
Cruel little mouth
(as my mother would say)
sucking on a lemon
and spitting out the pips
like short, cutting words,
embedded into my skin
like a christingle.

His eyes are too close
either side of his nose.
He leers at me
with his arm draped around you
like Red Riding Hood's cape,
taking a butcher's at the meat
sitting opposite him, oval gape.
He reminds me of the wolf
I have waiting at home.

The Contortionist

although my face
has mastered the art
of changing shape
I still can't find a way
to change your judgment of me
your little box of preconceived
memories and inconsistencies
the sober virgin
writing poetry on a bridge
wanting to be like you
because who wouldn't
want your lips to speak from
for just a moment
no one wants chapped lips
that study Philosophy
or eyes that prefer window seats
or hearts that need a little time
to breathe
except me
accept me
and remind me not to bite my nails

Shower Sessions

You're in the way of something,
standing between me and
the free fall.
The water's getting colder by the minute
and filling the smooth spaces between my toes.
I press my ear against the tiles
and hear music,
trapped in the bathroom of a house party.
Never invited,
not politely at least.
Thump thump,
noises from video games
and white, hard snow beneath my feet.
The tap drips,
video game shifts
inside screens
and exploding cables
electrify in the bathtub
and push neon colour into the soap bubbles.
Have you ever been high in the shower
and cried over the transparency of water?

Pillowcases

I never understood how it worked.
Press the blade in deep,
break skin and watch
the small seam of blood
open up with
flushes of red
in the bathtub.
Let the ruby streams
stain skin like rain
because rain only falls
on dark days.

Nuits Fauves

You travel to Paris on a whim
with a 35mm film camera
swinging from your slim neck
and a friend who applies her lipstick
looking into a silver teaspoon.

You dance in bars with older men
who mock your accent
and sweat attractively in the August heat,
smoke a pack of Camels,
buy a €4 rose on the street.

You eat snails,
ride the Metro,
and hold hands with a man
who speaks little English,
while picking tobacco
from beneath your fingernails.

You place the cigarette between your lips
and breathe it all in.

The Current

I found a crumb
in the carpet
rough and prickly
flicked it away
and returned to running my hand
through the tall thread
a sheet of ice atop this sea bed
pulling my feet in from the water and onto the rug
as I begin to think about rivers again
and how enraging it must be to follow
the path everyone else is taking
not enough power to burst the banks on your own
working in a supermarket with your mother
trading paint splattered overalls
for blood soaked scrubs
because Daddy doesn't like your paintings
too sentimental, too cliché
too easily flicked away

The Spill

I poured poetry into losing you
like I do everything else.
A beautiful and clammy spill
of irrational logic
and cold sentimentality.
I wrote expressions into your face
and read them back to front,
because how
after all this time
of examining your being
and settling myself within the cracks
could you no longer love me?
When I gave everything,
a one-sided,
all or nothing,
rage of love
met by your cool waves.
You put me out,
put me down
and smiled.
Maybe it was always only me
who saw the artistic beauty
in what we had.
Stupid boy,
you'll regret letting so much culture
slip from your veins
and back into mine.
Clearly you were empty
from the start,
a glass-never-full
kinda guy.

I Know Why

Apparently,
we can be wild
in the birdcage.
We can fly
sufficiently.
We can live
moderately.
We are free
in this new age
of clipped wings
and bird ringing.
We can adapt
adjust
acclimatise
to the heat of
the metal cage,
left in the
midday sun.

Cutthroat

they will be gritty
knives, forks and such
scraping their plates
serviettes and smudges
at the corners of their mouths

sit down slowly
don't rush the gentle art
of being civilised
don't speak about your interests
like they're interested

smile with your mouth shut
just enough to make them squirm
apply a little pressure
let the blood soak
through your napkin

compliment the decor
undermine them gradually
blink with big bloodshot eyes
and do your research
water the dead plant

this is how you get by
this is how you get by

Heavy

The flesh swells
beneath my fingernails,
until they burst out
from the thin, white frames
of skin that surround them.
My fingers fatten,
oozing out into my palms
until my hands are heavy
and the weight
tears through the seams
in my pockets,
fingertips brushing
muddy earth,
a buildup of dirt and ink.
I cannot write.
I cannot write.
No, never again.

The Wheel

I won't deny my doubts
or the fears I balance
on pinkie fingers
spinning the love
wrapped in the tough
cord of your body
not sure anymore
if I can keep breathing
these dreams like air
if they keep sticking to our lips like this
writing scripts like this
of loving you
but I've seen them pluck birds from the sky
and fish from the sea
so surely it could be easy for you and me
to stay in love for a little while longer

Cobblers

I used to wear red boots
and long checked shirts.
I was certain
and detailed
and read less
than I claimed I did.
I was tall
and concertinaed
so I always bounced back
into the arms that dropped me.
I painted poorly
and was proud,
wrote badly
and ripped spines
out of books that
I loved.
I bought expensive
shampoo
and spent a month
pulling out my hair
and hiding it in my desk.
I didn't exercise
or smile very often,
took pills instead.
I haven't changed much,
except
I wear green boots these days.

1929

Love the people with tea-stained faces
dripping with heirloom jewellery,
those who have bitten into life
with such might
that now their jaws are swollen.

For Frances

A twist in the globe of her hips
spins the leg
and screws her foot into position.
She bounces, springs into the dimly-lit sky
muffled with cloudy blemishes.
Her hair catches on the first light of 7pm stars,
glitter glinting between golden strands.
She laughs,
so big and brutal
that it breaks her skin a little.
Her toes skim the waves,
a transparent gloss coats her foot
up to her ankle,
before rejoining the sea.
She splashes, leans back and spins,
doubling the moon.
A movement recorded only by
the sand she stands in
and these words I write now.

Centre Court

my eyes flutter
blur
small green seed flies across the screen
heavy breathing suspended in sun beams
green pea
bouncing off tight strings
skimming the net
with a roar, a mighty scream
      IN
strong legs, thighs
shoes dug into soft earth
these women
with their sharp cheeks
that scrape the breeze
run alongside the sun
white, green
me
on the sofa
      OUT
watching the rhythm
the beat
forgetting
wishing my life was
as clean, as crisp, as free

Blue

there's no excuse
for listening to Joni Mitchell
on a rainy day
it's like running a hot bath
in summer
telling yourself
the more you burn
the deeper shade of
red you'll become
and red is the colour
of romance and love
so surely it will come
to me
if I just sit and bleed in the bath
thinking of you
and wondering why Joni chose blue

Borneo

The rain here is something wonderful and scary.
God has thrown a bucket of nails on the tin roof,
and waits for us to build something;
a wall to stop a landslide from flattening the village
and the children with drums and round stomachs.
Their smooth heads silhouette
against the violet sunset
and their small bodies wriggle into wheelbarrows,
back and forth between the mud piles
and the shacks standing at half mast.
Insects hang stagnant in the air
and scratch my throat
or crunch beneath my feet.
Brown dogs fight and threaten and mate.
I dig my nails into the tangle of twine
between my feet,
separate the lonely wild
from the peace I find here.
The teeth from the gum.

Strays

This beaten dog
won't get me
with its heavy eyes,
with its broken tail,
with its ribcage.

I made music
beating my own
bones,
pummelling my own chest.
I got something
to show for it.

I got hollow symphonies
and a shack for a home.

I owe the hound nothing.

We both howl for affection.
We both chase the bone.

Loser

If I could do it all again
I'd still kiss you by the tennis court
with my eye on the end
I would spend
each night
by your side
telling lies about our future
I would watch 'beautiful' form in your mouth
and deny it again
defy you again
give my all to you again
I'd give you the knife to make the scars
and the tongue to make the words
and feel the fall twice as hard
this broken thing would still run to you
and scrape her knees on your shoes
knowing she would
always
always
lose

Street Fighting

I make
round sounds
in little mouths
on stages too big
for subtle words but
I'm not your entertainment tonight folks
just a filler between acts
I'll step back as they begin
lift my chin
and raise my voice a little so you can hear me
I write poetry don't you know
        POETRY POETRY
that doesn't belong on the boulevard

Her Again

On the back foot,
a bloodied stump,
a crimson club
to thwack you with.
Hold it horizontal
across the door.
You will not touch her again.

Up against the wall,
terracotta brick,
a rough wound
and skin to peel back.
A gory mat
to pull from underneath you.
You will not touch her again.

A split lip,
a scarlet rip
dripping down her chin,
pooling in her
carved out collarbones.
A bare chest of bronze plated skin.
You will not touch her again.

The Student Life

They want to take me away
to a city I've only seen on TV,
and it all looks so big on such a small screen.
They want me to live in a flat
with people who have uneven personalities,
who will widen my horizons
that only stretch to the eastern coastline.
They want me on my knees,
they want to see me bleed
a little
into the concrete,
hold my forehead against the high-rise
and let the cold creep in
for the night.
They want to harden me,
knuckles knocked red
into the side of a man's cheek
who didn't even try to get to know me
before touching.
They want me to taste everything
and clink the chipped wine glasses,
shot glasses,
pass classes
and attend my graduation with a smile.
They want me to tell them it was worth it,
all the debt and the dirty stains.
They want me to throw the cap
and not take someone's eye out on the way.

The Commute

Bus driver's hungry grin,
sunken eyes like potholes.
He brushes my hand as
he takes the ticket,
inspects my clothes
and waits for my compulsory
closed-mouth smile.
The doors hold open,
my eyes are steely
and my hands are cold.
"You should smile, love,"
smoker's voice like an engine.
He hands me my ticket,
teeth gritted
I sit on the second deck.
I ignore the sign
and put my muddy shoes
on the seat opposite.
Stamp the dirt in.

Island

I sleep
and I am numb.
When did sleep become
the wave you chase
that never comes,
just retreats and runs,
touches the backlit sun
and leaves your feet dry?
When did the bed grow?
Did it soak in the warmth
by the window and swell?
Ping the sheets from the corners,
stretch its legs.
When did I start feeling so lonely?
Was it when I reached for you
and felt nothing but a shore,
felt nothing but the cold sheet?
Washed up on an island,
where you no longer love me.

Disconnected

I'm at the end of my rope,
you're on the end of the line
and you have no clue
because I've hidden them all.
"I guess I should let you go,"
flies over your head and into my eyes.
I rub it out
and tears scale down.
It's all over isn't it?
And your only crime
is that smile that stops me
from saying goodbye.

On My Mind at 2am

Is it happy?
Is it running deep
inside little houses,
little mouses
and all the little things
we were told about
as children?

Does it fall?
Does it watch our
last performance
with awe
and throw roses onto
the stage?

Or does it rage,
does it boo,
spit,
leave through the backdoor?
Dead lovers crying
in an empty theatre.

Is it fresh?
Does it bleed
new
each day
and stain the
wine glasses?

I hope it's ripe,
I hope it hurts
in the night.
I hope it heals,
but long before you do.

I hope it sees me
in the city,
with someone new

smiling.
I hope it wants me
to look back,
and I hope I never do.

Flutter

She is black and blue all over,
a bright bruise
in the queue to the nightclub.
Moth grey eyeshadow,
fragile thin wings
don't feel a thing,
dressed down for the night
as a butterfly.
She sings,
hear her night call,
she sings.

A Hungry Man Am I

A hungry man am I,
a fatty belly never full.
I push it out, rub it,
stuff it with juicy people.
Feed my appetite
with your warm touches
and hot glances.
I will lick you up
off the floor.
I will take what I can get.
There will never be enough
breath in my lungs to satisfy,
unless it is emptied
from in between your words,
sucking out the spaces like sherbet.
Your starving, skinny sentences
spat out onto the dining table.
I will gobble it up,
I will eat up all this love.

For Keats

Art was all that was in him,
even his face
framed
by a dark border of curls
and his fingers shaped to hold a pen,
a brush,
a lady's soft hand.
He paused often,
took his time among the flowers
and the hills that would rupture beneath his feet.
He wrote beside the window,
watched the ledge collect leaves, snow,
white like snowflaked skin,
as seasons changed and aged.
When he died,
everything stopped trying
and nothing grew for months.
We all starved
and that was the only fair part
about any of it.

Raise

lay flowers at the foot of my grace
find the feint line
between my beauty
and my vices
hold the gate open
and let them flood
into the places
I protect with
empty sentences
let's unpick the stitches together
and watch it all fall in on itself
I promise you won't forget the sight
of a girl razed to the ground

Fingerprints

You talked about staying pregnant forever,
your womb a little coat of armour
which sadness couldn't dent
and life couldn't bend
to its will,
if you just remained still
and held onto your baby
over the years.
No childhood fear or trauma,
just a little warmer
than the chill out here.
But love is not bulletproof
and neither is a shield of skin.
It wasn't your fault
that the rain poured in
and lack of sleep or salad
was not the cause,
I promise he felt your warmth
before leaving.
He felt you breathing
and knew you as his mother.

Back and Forth

A whelk dug deep into
the low tide sands,
pushed
sharply down and in,
I have changed a thing
on this beach
with my hand.
As the sea creeps forward,
fish will swim,
waves will roll over,
crabs will totter by
my installation,
"anything can be called art these days,"
they will say
dislodging the shell,
watching it get carried away
again.

Train Stations

Maybe we'll meet again
when the trees stop rushing past the windows
and I stop dancing with this stranger
who holds my body like it's hollow.

Except from the strings of sentences
that hang loosely like bunting in my head.
He spins me and jumbles up all the letters.
I'll leave him soon I think,
when the words begin to rhyme again.

Salsa Class

I'm smiling
the way a person smiles
when they've found something new
to fall into
not a man
or a bottle
but a pair of hands
to hold loosely
and arms to move through
to a Cuban beat
and palms to touch
    meet
and part
a stranger's grip
and smiles across the room
stepping back and forth
not thinking of you
for a while
and instead
spending the evening
dancing

2018

This year.
What year?
Who yearns for the skinning?
Shedding days like
dollar signs from the back of the billionaire
and promising ourselves
that we can be better but
no one will notice.
No one will care.

August

Meat cleaver cut face
mottled with red,
full and heavy,
a salty weight.
Will it always be her?
Every time?
Every summer?

Pinhole pricked throat,
nailing voice,
hammer, screwdriver,
bricked up little mouth.
Will it always be her
who you leave me
in the rain for?

Wet cheeks tucked
under my eyes,
pinched nose, damp hair,
still   still crying.
Will it always be her?
Eyes bright, cheeks blushed,
still   still laughing.

Fashionably Late

I am back again
beckoning you with my tongue,
pushing you down onto your knees with a stare.
You grasp for the air between my legs when I walk.
I circle the room like a minute hand,
arrive late
and in love
but non-committal.
My glass is full
and my belt-buckle gleams bright.
You wait for my next move.
Tonight's the night.

Closure

you didn't have the energy
to wrap up GOODBYE
and send it to me
I know it's late
but it still gets to me
that you don't want to text me
at three
in the morning
when you can see
my knees bleeding
in front of you
kissing your feet
and alone
because we never said goodbye
just stopped saying hello

Heat Wave

you come to sleep on my bedroom floor
lay your weighted head on the coarse carpet
strip clothes from your back
you say it's too hot in your room
no windows to let the new day through
the fan twists
moves your hair
moves mine
your bare body crawls away from itself
skin peeling from bone
entering its own cool space
as the moth tattoo on your back
spreads it's stiff wings against your shoulder blades
I look up through the skylight
clouds lay flat against the houses
trapping the heat between us
as blue tack slacks and posters fall from the walls
eyes sting in the insomnia
sweat seals my body to the sheets
but you lay asleep
hair stuck to your forehead
eyes flickering in arctic dreams

A Design Flaw

I don't miss you,
per se
but holding a man in bed
is always a nice way to end the day.
All those limbs,
skin on skin
in a wooden twin bed.
A chest as a pillow,
a toned torso,
someone should sell it
on Dragons' Den.
I'd buy one
but then again,
would it be the same
without him saying my name
through the night?
Over and over
into the night.

Animals

I don't mind listening to false talk
on a Friday night
with friends who hang from
my shoulder blades
like apes
and whisper cold things with hot breath
into ears.

I don't mind smoking by the backdoor
with the TV on so loudly,
I can hear it from outside:
missiles, stabbings, suicide,
from the pretty reporter in red,
who grits her teeth until
the camera stops rolling.

I don't mind listening to my sister cry
over the phone with wet lips
and a slippery voice
that falls over itself
and into his arms
again
and again.

I don't mind anything at all really,
I don't have the time.

Missing You

When hours started weighing like
second-shaped stones
upon my head,
I knew you had me tied tight
between your fingers,
between your lungs
beat
beating
like the hands of a clock
that must wait to touch you.

The Creative

I want to create something
that matters
even though
I'll never know if it should
or if I'm just a girl who could
never get attention with her looks
so she searches for it on paper instead
and hates her chest
when no one bothers to notice.
Writing poems at a time
when the world has no time at all
and not a second to spare for truth.
I just want to hold onto my youth
and write lines
that make people cry.
I think that says a lot about me.
It says all the things that I would
never dare write down,
ironically.

Family Reunion

The people in my family are unreasonable.
Their jaws are clenched too tight
and they only uncurl their fists after 7pm
and a few pints.
They judge behind backs because it's easier that way
and shake their heads too many times a day
about things they know don't matter.

The people in my family are controlling.
I have seen manipulation in so many shapes
that I no longer believe it has one,
just a shiftless and clever thing
that scares us into silence.

The people in my family are unreliable.
They promise and backtrack and doubt their own feelings
because 'healing' isn't a word we use very often.

The people in my family
are hard, soft,
never enough,
too much
and estranged from someone they love.
But, oh how they love
and are desperate to stay,
to stay alive
for one more night,
one more fight
behind my grandparents' house
that we'll laugh about in years to come.

The Ledge

Can you step back for a moment
and take it all in
while I run thin
on emotions
and tell lies about my little life
like long words and titles matter
to people with eyes
that can see above the windowsill?
And don't feel obliged
to lift me high,
I'll just complain that
you're holding onto me too tight.
I'm like that, you know.
I'll take it out on you
because you'll be close
and kind enough
to bear it
and judge me quietly.
Just don't tell me politely
when you decide to leave,
although I won't see it coming:
not quite tall enough to see.

Pixels

it's Friday night
and there's no one home
my toes are cold
because it's May
and no one wants to face
that we still need the heating on
still need to keep keeping on
and writing poetry
that no one cares about
writing my cares out
and foolishly calling them revolutionary
watching grainy Bukowski
interviews in bed
comparing the size of his head
to mine
thinking about what's inside
thinking if maybe in some way
we thought the same
preferred the same shade of green
or supported the same sports team
maybe
that 99.9% gene similarity
is all I need to convince myself
that I could be as great as the ones
who are far greater than me

Margaret

She is fed with a plastic spoon.
She bites her lip
and it bleeds pink.
She is fed
    fed.

She is entertained with felt
and pencils,
blunt and safe.
She is entertained
    entertained.

She is lowered into the bed,
into the grave
by four twenty-somethings.
She is lowered
    lowered.

Mrs Atlantic

call upon the god
Mrs Atlantic
treading water
slamming the souls of her feet
against the sharp blue

lips resting atop the waves
calling for you to
stop messing around
stop wasting your life
on boring men
and mundane TV shows
that make you fantasise
about another boring man

she is drowning for you
letting the salt bubbles
lift her lungs into her throat
as you refuse to breathe in
avoiding second-hand smoke
and male musk

get over yourself
she is dying
while you spend another
evening at home
with another book in your dry
uncomfortable hands
that have never kept
a tight grip on anything
slipped from passion to passion
lover to lover
sea to sea

she sinks
and you blink
in your boredom
watch the dull colours

move under your eyelids
like the northern lights
that you will never bother
to get up and see

No Lies

We are ravaged daily
by harsh light and weather,
by the sharp teeth they sew into our shoes,
by loneliness,
by the gaping holes in our roofs
and the mouldy mouths of damp on the ceiling,
by feeling
and by the sight of swollen lips
on past lovers.

Play Fighting

We had some ideas
and then sent them to war
because that's what thoughts
and minds are for, right?
Never giving up the fight,
never seeing the sight
that gave us light in the first place.
Just battles,
just shackles,
just wrists and ankles
perfectly sculpted for chains,
and brains on the canvas
and blood on the atlas.
Lightbulb mouths reduced
to siren sounds
and shrapnel in skin
and things that dig in,
things the Westerner can't imagine.
Because on that field
with the girls and boys
and their trigger-finger pleasing toys,
you can't hear the cries
of a toddler under rubble.

Detour

I want to sink into your mind
like hands into sand,
change your plans
and carve crescent moons
from your kneecaps.

The Hill

Someone once told me
that only the lonely
go to Paris in love.
No lip locking,
no keys under
welcome mats,
just you,
the streets
and the Louvre.
A rose in a glass
and a fierce rebellion in a bottle,
passion in every shade of red,
a passion for poetry,
a passion for moonlight on girls' faces
and bicycles with baskets.
People in Paris
fall in love with Paris
and leave
knowing they will never love another
with all their heart
because Paris stole a piece at
Montmartre.

Vamps

I spent last night
in the corner of an ugly room
with a boy who liked my eyes
and sucked my neck
until he got bored
and sat on the windowsill to smoke
someone told me to smile
so I bit them
and they left me well alone for the rest of the night
warning people about the girl
with the green eyes and the strong jaw

The Second Child

I've abandoned you before,
been angry
and lost sight of things.
I blinded myself to spite you,
bumped into you
and then asked why you were bruised.
I blamed you
and ripped heart-shaped holes into your paintings
then hid the gaps with pages of my poetry.
"Look at me Mummy,
I can be just as gifted"
even if I have to try,
even if it doesn't come naturally
or flow from my bones.
I'm sorry that I resented you,
I didn't mean it,
I just slipped into it
like a pair of your hand-me-down jeans.

Slice

names
dates
record players
fate

so many things spinning
like fingertips
on ice rinks

Beginnings

our end
wasn't mine
not in the slightest
I've still got the bite just
not the bark
anymore
I don't need it
when the words speak for me
and I can let the things that bore me
just slip on by
along with your smiles that unsettled me
and the bed you made just so
sheets neatly nipped in
I always got under them
and under your skin
kicked frantically
dipped my toe in
until you splashed me
but now I'm swimming
and the water is so much clearer
and I can finally breathe deeper
without fear of the under current
without waves tying me
to a me that died a long time ago
a dead weight
that you can keep
or clip to your rearview mirror
if you wish
because our end
wasn't mine
not in the slightest

Circus

The freak,
the maddened beast
against the bars,
does he rattle you
in his face paint
and war scars?
Does he remind you
of the dog you have
chained up in the yard?
Does he lick his
wounds so lightly that
you mistake them for yours?

Gallery

I want this
you
me
suffocated
in each other's company
a hand on my waist
and a hum in my hair
time to spare
time
   S
      L
         O
           W
              E
                D
down
and clothes that adorn the floor
like modern art
the pillows
are goose feather
and the feeling
is deep
I'm breathing in you
and you're choking on me

(you need some water, baby?)

Desdemona

I'm sorry about all of this;
all this blood I've spilled
with butter fingers,
slipping and sliding across
the hallway
in these ruby slippers
and falling into your scarlet stream
with greedy thoughts.
What a mess I've made!
I've given the game away,
and the next time you bring her
through the backdoor
to your bedroom,
she'll see the red curtains,
watch the flags flutter
and know.
Us girls have a taste for it.
Blood on bed sheets,
is that all we are to you now?

White Moth

I may be having an identity crisis
or just noticing an overlap in the chain
a neat flap of skin from the base of my fingernail
lapping up my left brain
like a dog at his water bowl
staring at his reflection
and not seeing himself

I am, I am the same
but changed
twisted at the waist
watching my back in the mirror
as skin wastes away from the mountain ridge
that stops me folding in on myself
upside down
bumping noses with a stranger

eyes adjusted to the size of shadow men
that seek me out
teeth bared for the hunt
for the white moth in their peripheral
for the cheap smell

I am the flower
that reads Plath
and the slut
that howls Bukowski
watching her face move in the mirror
and wondering why this lonely woman
stands so far back from me

To Our Parents

What have you left my children?
A grape, a rotten core?
A planet twisted, bunched,
punched clean of its blue and green?
A broken toy on the cracked concrete?
A slim slice of wonder
in the occasional tree they see?
Something sharp enough to cut through the hunger,
to cut the skin from their backs with each degree?
What have you left my children?
A gasp of grey breath?
A blindfold by an open fire?
An inherited death?

Nest

You gonna box up?
Cardboard cuts as you fill up,
grow up,
move on
and out of me.
You're a big boy,
not my baby
any more.
So I'll watch over the town for you,
keep shit pinned down for you,
stay in touch with your mother
and call you at night
when the time's right
and you need space from
the new crowd.
I'll remind you of what
my house looks like
in winter
and I'll frame it up real nice.
So get up,
move on
and out of me.
We were perfect firsts
but future's the charm
and I'm not gonna keep you back from that,
trap you,
shackle you to me
when we were only meant to be
temporary lovers.
So step up,
move on,
you'll know where to find me.

Forecast

I'm still waiting for that day,
when an eclipse comes without warning
and you uncoil from my finger
without turning around to say goodbye.

I can feel it brewing like thunder storms,
shaking the clouds above my house
and throwing picture frames from the wall,
but no one says a word.

The clock hides time with its hands
and the days peel away from me like paint.
Please just tell me when it ends,
tell me when the next sunrise will be our last
so I don't take it all for granted.

3 / 6

I wish I had as much to say
as the old ladies on the bus
with plastic around their heads,
protecting thin hair from the rain.
Backs of fingers
rub murky windows clear,
glimpsing out into a square of world
like it's the only part that matters.
Wrap your scarves a little tighter please,
staying warm is a necessity
and it's something that we're losing,
slowly
surely.

The Deep End

I'm at the bottom of the bed
ship wrecked
as your hands sail across
creased sheets
to reach me
pull me from my peace
make sure you didn't leave
anything behind
dig your fingers
into the folds in my chest
tear it apart
denting the gold
bending the silver
ripping copper strands
from my head
lower the mast darling
I'm done
take it all
thank God
you sunk me here
a bed
a sea
that might just
carry me away
from you
in the morning

The Secret

here he is
wearing his smile
like it's foreplay
hair pushed back into days
we spent learning from each other's bodies
and hating each other's tongues
spending mornings
counting the cracks in his ceilings
his walls
and the noisy bed frame
always the same
disappointed look
when he sees the
eyeshadow stains on the sheets
but I knew he'd be washing them anyway
the moment I leave

For The Lion At The Museum

You're like me at parties
maybe,
in a place you don't belong.
People move past you,
King of the Jungle,
as their phones light up their faces,
leaving you in shadow
as you wait between sheets of glass
alone.
Eyes foggy and teeth blunt now,
clawless and soft now,
empty like a swollen belly in the desert,
watched like a girl in the city
as your kingdom is torn from its bed
and the leaves fall in mourning
five thousand miles away.
I weep for you
and all your fading glory.

Stick

She never stood a chance,
planted deep into the roots of the country that watered
but never fed her,
filling her bowl with spaghetti women
that slip through her fingers
and through the gaps between her teeth
each time she tries to swallow.

Her eyes glaze over all
those lava lamp ladies,
hot and swelling,
that glow in the corner of dark rooms,
luscious colour running along the seams of their skin
and spilling out
and into cracks in the wooden floor.

So she lets her body wilt
and skins fruit with the blunt ends of her teeth,
curling spirals onto her tongue
like pencil sharpenings.
They crawl down into her stomach
as the apple core hourglass waits
and counts time
and the bathroom tiles
she'll be lying on in the morning.

Star-Crossed

like spacemen lost in slow steps
I'm forever avoiding craters to reach you
finding spots in your sunset
and pulling them open
like oranges in fruit bowls
hoping the colour will fill me up
and pierce my skin
paper lantern hearts trying to find each other
and taping 'missing' signs to lampposts

Rouge

let's call ourselves artists
and write poetry in Paris
pillaging padlocks on bridges
and kissing beneath them
our red skin raging under moonlight
and stumbling through streets
in drunken clarity
hold it gently
and take a piece of the revolution
when you leave

Nocturnal

Your chin sinks into the pillow,
eyelashes flickering against the cotton.
You are a sleepy man,
a night owl
with a 5AM alarm.
You are working before the birds sing.
You are breathless by the morning.
You twist your body,
upright against the headboard,
watching my silhouette soak through the shower curtain
like ink on blotting paper.
You wait for me before you sleep.
A book lies open in both your hands,
vulnerable and happy,
as the corners of your mouth twitch
with each word.
You barely notice me
slip under the covers.
Every night is like the first night;
you switch off the light,
watch dark forms move in the blackness,
pay attention to every second of your life,
every line on my palm,
every death.
Sleep doesn't find you easily,
you're always hiding at midnight.

Drunk

I think I drank the sea last night.
The waves still rock inside my stomach
as the tide pushes me forward,
then pulls me back into sickness
and kitchen floors.
I just wanted to have dinner with you,
but the cool air by the beach
was a little too potent,
and the water
was a little too choppy,
and it seems I got lost again.

4 Months Later

Waiting in your cafe,
our cafe
once.
Chimes from china teacups
coming from behind the counter,
clinks marking moments like coffee stains
on blouses
that remind me of that afternoon
where clumsy, nervous hands spilled
as you walked in.
It was embarrassing
but you didn't seem to mind
once upon a time.

And now I wait again.
It's a clever game you play
as I lock down my restless legs
that itch to stand up to greet you.
But today is a new kind
that calls for a warm face
that makes you feel cold
and fill the chill with hot coffee.

You're anxious,
you see how easily I can read
between the lines by your mouth
as you sip.
"I'm doing very well," you say;
I nod and don't mention
what your sister told me
last week.

I resist the urge to list my new achievements
on my lipstick pressed napkin,
tell you how well I'm doing
in my newly-single, decaffeinated life.
But I just smile,
bringing the cup to my lips

with my upper-hand
and watch you stumble over excuses to see me,
but I've got a lot on you see
and these days I'm just far too busy
for this,
for you,
for coffee.

Loophole

Don't let
your words
walk the streets
alone at night.
It's a dangerous place
for sweet nothings
and it will always
be their fault
when someone else
reads them
wrong.

Time

I know we're tired of
twiddling hitchhikers' thumbs
living in bloated, empty houses
and finding new ways to say "I love you"
but give us time
we have an age of
breathing and teething
and finding life's meaning
brushing lips
as we hang from the cliff's edge
fingers dug deep into time
passing seconds back and forth
like a wine
bottle
perched on the curb
and singing
don't race me
or chase me
to the finish line
when we have all this time

Ten Pin

Glitter gutted
heavy eyelids
blinking in bowling allies,
hot and clammy
lips in gloss,
Kate Moss
on her t-shirt.
Long legs straddling laps
of boys she can't stand
so fuck the patriarchy,
funk in the dance party,
quoting Gandhi in the caption
of her mirror selfie.
You smiling at me,
or the guy on TV
with the hair
and white teeth?
He can't see you,
you know,
none of us can.

The Bear

Take your shoes off by the door,
watch the dogs pant in the heat,
and forget the day you saw your mother cry for the first time.
She has cried every day since you were born
and your father has been fearful for a long time.
Separate the tens from the twenties,
stack them,
pay your debts.

I watched an old friend burn a book on a bonfire
and slap the dirt from his feet with an open palm.
"I run better without shoes."
He wraps the laces round his wrists, ankles, neck,
he twists, pretends to strangle himself.
He laughs.
He keeps his cash behind a wooden mask mounted on his wall.
His runaway money for a car, a plane ticket.
His new shoe fund.

New Year's

last year
finger tapping
on glass bottles
to lazy beats
confetti on the floor
sparks in the sky
your lips wrapped
into a smile
unkissed
hearts in need
of warmth
chapped lips
numb fingers
empty glasses

tonight I will
soak your lips
in wine
and your fingers
will sleep in my hair
we will save
the year
before it has
begun
and I will wipe clean
the last 365 days
with my tongue

let's start again
3, 2, 1...

Bled Dry

You call just before midnight
and ask me to tie up your hair
and wash your back in the bath.
You tell me blood only makes us sisters
in that paper thin,
cut and torn
kind of way,
but we deserve the name
because we've
cut down the trees
in our own back gardens
to give the poets something to write on.

The Shallow

I wish it flowed deeper
and I wasn't so alone in this endless blue.
I wish these clothes weren't empty
and these words weren't cruel,
but they are.
So I'm tiptoeing across your bedsheets
and waiting for my next lover
because blue was never my colour
and it was never yours either.

14/02

You slept with her on Valentine's Day
but said it didn't count because you were high.
Pointed tip-toed feet slicing through clouds
as you crept around up there,
tightening your tie around the doorknob
with swollen lips,
lifting you further up like pink balloons
and soon you'll be bumping into the moon
and bullshitting the stars too.

5pm

I walk home
pressing stones
into the bottom of my shoes.
Hungry for food
and love
and everything in between.
I see the pink glow above the trees.
I wonder if it's the sunset,
I wonder if it's a fire,
I wonder about you and me.

Her Hands

I've tried to write so many poems
for my Mother
to make her heart flutter
and ease her soul a little
but they are never right
always a mile off being light enough
to express her blinding love
as all encompassing
as the time in a pocket watch
kept safe in her hand
as she uses the other to hold all the things
you never knew were yours to carry
because she never complains about the weight
she just stays up late and paints
lonely, holy figures
as I sleep
and thank God
she'll be there to wake me
in the morning

The Suburbs of Paris

scrape your shoes against their houses
kick the curb
squeeze your stomachs until they pop
maybe the sound will wake them
there's graffiti on the cars
and you paint in blues and reds
salt water still soaks you
but the boats are long gone
wrap your teeth around the wheels of their white cars
beep your horn
and scream through the window
because there's graffiti on the cars
and still no one listens

On The Lake

I am alive,
pale blue
and singing from the lips.
Dragged from the surface shatter,
from the midnight shutters
of the water,
black and deep
and flowing up from my lungs
like blood in the moonlight.
Lids heavy but risen,
staring up at a disapproving sky,
vibrating and buzzing
as my body shivers, quivers
from the pitch reflection of the mirror,
rippling against the current.
A hungry river
clawing out,
ripping my trouser leg,
it wants me asleep on its rocky bed
tonight.
But I am alive,
pale blue
and in the arms of a rambling stranger,
slapping my cheeks,
rousing red,
the colour of DANGER DANGER DANGER.
Do not warm me with stinking bodies
that raise my wet back from the ground.
This wan swan must swim tonight,
she swims, she kicks, she

drowns.

Maya Elphick

Maya Elphick is a poet, writer and English Literature student from Norfolk in the UK. She has been publishing poetry on her Instagram page @m.g.petri since 2017 and her work has featured in three poetry anthologies. This is Maya's first book of poetry.

Printed in Poland
by Amazon Fulfillment
Poland Sp. z o.o., Wrocław

51004182R00082

Beyond Busyness

Time Wisdom in an Hour

STEPHEN CHERRY

Sacristy Press
PO Box 612, Durham, DH1 9HT

www.sacristy.co.uk

First published in 2013 by Sacristy Press, Durham

Sacristy Limited, registered in England
& Wales, number 7565667

British Library Cataloguing-in-Publication Data
A catalogue record for the book is available
from the British Library

ISBN 978-1-908381-13-2

This book began life in February 2013 when I issued the challenge to "Give up busyness for Lent". This "I'M NOT BUSY" campaign was largely a social media phenomenon, and people who took it on reported that it was a real and deep struggle, but that as they stayed with it so their life began to change—and much for the better.

My challenge to give up busyness has now moved on from "for Lent" to "for Life". The website (**www.notbusy.co.uk**) will remain an online source of ideas and encouragement for people who decide to respond to the challenge, and the publisher has made a range of items available to help and encourage people on this quest for a more measured and balanced pace of life.

Although my first book in this area was intended to help clergy and others engaged in ministry it found a much wider audience. This book, however, is intended for people of any faith or none and is designed so that it can be read within an hour.

However, without the support and encouragement of those who took on the challenge for Lent 2013, this project would never have got off the ground, and so **I dedicate this little book to everyone who gave up busyness (with whatever degree of success) in Lent 2013.**

Contents

PART 1

Before You Begin

Okay, you are busy, so let's not waste any time on an introduction.

Spend no more than two minutes looking down the following list and decide which of these statements apply to you:

- I often feel that there is not enough time.
- I often work more hours than I should.
- Days off can feel as if they are adding time pressure.
- My family miss out on my time because of other demands.
- I spend too much time on admin.
- I do not take all of my holiday entitlement.
- I wish I had fewer meetings.
- I sometimes realise too late that I have missed a great opportunity.
- Time pressures make it difficult or impossible for me to live up to my own expectations as a warm and caring person.
- When people say, "how are you?" I often reply, "busy".

So, how many of these apply?

If it is five or more . . . Bingo! This book is for you.

PART 2

"New Busy" or "The Busyness Syndrome"

I can't say exactly when it happened, but at some point in recent years the word "busy" changed its meaning. Once upon a time it meant, "I have rather more to do at the moment than usual, and I am not sure whether I am going to get it all done—but that's all part of the fun of life". Those were the days when the word "busy" had a smile on its face. Today "busy" has lost its smile and its meaning is more ambiguous. This book is *not* designed to eliminate the experience of busy from your life. It *is* designed to put a smile back on the face of busy.

In order to do that we need to say more about what the word "busy" has come to mean.

Have you noticed how many people give you the answer "busy" when you ask them how they are or how things are going? Similarly, have you spotted that people now use the word "busy" both as a positive, even boastful, self-description ("look at me, I'm busy"), and yet at the same time hint that as they are busy they deserve a little of your sympathy? Today, the word "busy" wants to have its cake and eat it too.

Even worse, "busy" has become an excuse. It is used in such a way as to give the speaker an alibi for anything they have not done or do not intend to do. So when asked about something they promised to do people say something like, "I am sorry I have not done *that* [the word is weighted with a little implicit disdain] but I have been very busy".

What you are *not* allowed to say in response is, "I'm very sorry to hear that you have been busy, but I thought we agreed that this would be a priority for you".

If you did say it, this is perhaps how the conversation would develop:

"Oh, yes it was," says the busy person, "but there were so many things . . . I can't go through them all. I really was just too busy. But I will get on with it now, as the deadline is so close."

"The deadline has in fact passed".

"Well I will definitely get on with it then." (Thinks: "this is what is going to make me busy today. How exciting!")

You get the picture.

Another aspect of the new busy is that it applies as equally to leisure activities as it does to jobs that need to be done—whether at work or at home. **The new busy does not respect the distinction between essential and desirable.** This is one reason that the "two-column To Do list" (which will be explained in Part 6) can be such an effective weapon against busyness syndrome. It is also why people can be busy on holiday or on their days off. They really want to squeeze in the extra round of golf and are determined to get the children to yet another activity. Then they go and spoil it all by calling it "busy".

Some of the worst culprits for living lives of leisure but describing themselves as busy are the retired, or at least those who have been retired long enough to be able to say "I don't know how I had time to go to work" or "I have never been busier". We have all heard these comments, but few would dare to say, "ahem . . . I wonder how much of that busyness has the primary objective of enjoyment". Not a wise comment to make to your elders, perhaps, but if we invariably fail to challenge some of the uses to which the word "busy" is put today, then we will be colluding with the toxic effect it is having on our lives.

When people who live leisured lives begin to describe themselves as busy we know that something sinister has happened. A cultural line has been crossed and values have been reshaped. We have entered the unhealthy territory of the new busy; we are in the grip of the busyness syndrome.

The new busy, then, is a way of life in which people are driven by unmanageable demands. It is not an occasional state caused by a sudden change in circumstances or the onset of a specific crisis. It is a chronic condition, a disease. As soon as one thing goes, another replaces it. Whereas "old busy" would give us an adrenalin rush that would spice life up a bit, "new busy" exhausts us because we start to live off the adrenalin (or its tasty substitute, caffeine) and feel listless, wretched, pointless and mildly (or seriously) depressed when not being hyperactive.

OLD BUSY	NEW BUSY
Episodic	Chronic
Fuelled by the unexpected	Driven by the unmanageable
Exciting adrenalin rush	Exhausting adrenalin overload
One of those things	A source of pride, identity even
Product of events	Product of attitude
A genuine explanation given with regret and sincere apology	A ready-made excuse for not doing things
Could be minimised by better time management	Aggravated by time management

Figure 1: Table highlighting key differences between "old busy" which is a passing and transitional phase, and "new busy" which is a relentless state driven by internal as much as external factors.

In his short story *Crazy Busy*, Julian Boote paints a picture of social, ethical and civic breakdown caused by a time management application which goes viral.[1] This huge engine of productivity delivers highly satisfying rewards to people as they complete their next bit of work within an impossibly demanding deadline. They love it and inevitably get addicted. In no time at all people are transformed from happy workers to compulsive deadline-achievers. The pleasure of reward has morphed into the threat of non-reward. This is work-aholism cubed and it is the product of the most highly developed and efficient time management tool imaginable—a tool which treats people as machines and forgets about their deeper needs and resources. Time is treated like one long snake of moments which can be chopped into ever smaller sections, each one made more productive than the last.

As Boote's story suggests, busyness is not only a problem

[1] Julian Boote, *Crazy Busy* (2010); available as an e-book.

for individuals; it impacts businesses, corporations and institutions. I have certainly seen it happen around me in the places where I work. It is as if the corporate car only has one foot pedal. There is an accelerator but no clutch to help change gear (why change gear if you are going flat out?) and certainly no brake.

This metaphor was used in a groundbreaking article which appeared in the Harvard Business Review in 2010: it is called *The Acceleration Trap*.[2] This is how the authors, Heike Bruch and Jochen I. Menges, introduce the article and summarise the idea:

> Faced with intense market pressures, corporations often take on more than they can handle: they increase the number and speed of their activities, raise performance goals, shorten innovation cycles, and introduce new management technologies or organisational systems. For a while, they succeed brilliantly, but too often the CEO tries to make this furious pace the new normal. What began as an exceptional burst of achievement becomes chronic overloading, with dire consequences. Not only does the frenetic pace sap employee motivation, but the company's focus is scattered in various directions, which can confuse customers and threaten the brand.
>
> Realising something is amiss, leaders frequently try to fight the symptoms instead of the cause. Interpreting employees' lack of motivation as laziness or unjustified protest, for example, they increase the pressure, only making matters worse. Exhaustion and resignation begin to blanket the company, and the best employees defect.

---

[2] Heike Bruch and Jochen I. Menges, "The Acceleration Trap", in *Harvard Business Review*, April 2010.

Their research was based on more than 600 companies. Some they diagnosed as "fully trapped". In them, 60% of employees agreed or strongly agreed that they lacked sufficient resources to get their work done (whereas this was true for only 2% in companies that weren't trapped) and 80% said that they worked under "constant elevated time pressure".

The Acceleration Trap is the corporate version of the "busyness syndrome" as it afflicts individuals—the "new busy". The problem is not that there is sometimes the need for exceptional levels of activity and effort. It is that this becomes the new normal.

The article analyses the problem in terms of three patterns of destructive activity. While described in organisational language they will be familiar to anyone who has become busy in the new sense. First there is *overloading* – that is, being faced with more work than can be done. One company for instance doubled the value of its contracts without addressing capacity issues. Second there is *multiloading*, which means that people are asked to do too many different things. The consequence is that employees lack focus and activities are unaligned. You could think of this in terms of a lack of "joined-up-ness" or internal coherence. Third there is the pattern which they call *perpetual loading*, which is the habit of constantly imposed change. This, the authors suggest, leads to relentless and debilitating frenzy.

The Acceleration Trap is where companies get stuck if they try too hard for too long.

Oddly, the same thing can happen to people who have a significant degree of personal freedom and control over their own lives. What is different here is probably the hardest and strangest thing to understand. Unlike the Acceleration Trap which makes victims of employees, the new busy is less a product of events, and more a product of attitude. **New busy happens not because of things "out there", but because of things "in here".**

PART 3

Two Ironies

There are two things that fuel new busy more than anything else—time-saving devices and time management techniques. Our investment in time-saving gadgets and devices has increased exponentially over the years. The industrial revolution saw the beginning of it. This led in turn to the domestic revolution where machines were brought into the house to do the work. It moved on a leap or two with the invention of food processors and microwave ovens. More recently it has bounced forward into previously unimaginable everyday realities with the information technology revolution. All this could mean that we are able to get all our work done before lunch and spend the rest of the day in peaceful and enjoyable contemplation. On the contrary, we find more and more things to do and make ourselves busy in ways that our great grandparents would find utterly astonishing.

Many people who are caught up in the syndromes and sicknesses that are part and parcel of new busy are expert time managers. If they are the retired they will have learnt about time management at work, and they will have found ways of being ever more productive and effective. They may have helped others to do the same— looking for time-efficient ways of changing processes and practices. They will know about planning tools and will know how to manage their calendar and diary.

But time management, like all management, needs a framework within which to operate. It needs some overarching goals and values and priorities if it is not to become its own end.

"What are you doing?" "More with less."

"When are you doing it?" "Now!"

This might be the rallying call of time managers on the march. But it is a vapid and hopeless campaign. The interesting question is neither "How much are you going to do?" nor "How time efficiently are you going to do it?" Rather it is, "What purpose do you really want to serve?"

No time management book, system or process can help you answer this question. Indeed it is very likely to distract you from the necessary and probably rather slow task of working out your own position on just this issue—which is where time wisdom comes in.

PART 4
Time Wisdom

Time is a funny thing. It was St Augustine who put his finger on it in his *Confessions*. "Provided no one asks me, I know," he wrote, but, "if I want to explain to an enquirer, I do not know."[3] That sums it up for me! Stephen Hawking's *A Brief History of Time* was a bestseller, presumably because people felt that by reading it they would at last understand time. Many fell at the first equation and decided to waste no more time on trying to understand time. They were probably wise to recognise that the book was too difficult for them, but wrong to give up on trying understanding time.

It is a mystery, of course. We have difficulty conceiving anything beyond time and yet we also know that there was a time when time began. We are entirely comfortable with the idea of past, present and future but are hard pressed to know when the present moment begins or ends. How long is now? No one knows, and maybe different "nows" have different lengths.

The psychologists Philip Zimbardo and John Boyd write about *The Time Paradox* and suggest that there are six different time perspectives:[4]

---

[3] St Augustine, *Confessions* (4th cent.), ch. 11, sec. 14.
[4] Philip G. Zimbardo and John Boyd, *The Time Paradox: The New Psychology of Time That Will Change Your Life* (Free Press, 2008).

- past-negative
- present-hedonistic
- future
- past-positive
- present-fatalistic
- transcendental-future

They even offer a questionnaire to enable you to see how strong these perspectives are in your own experience of time. I have often done a little experiment with groups of people asking them to stand at one end of the room if they like the past, the other if they focus on the future and in the middle if the present moment is their thing. The hugely unscientific results often have a similar number of people in the past and the present, with relatively few having a future perspective. It would be interesting to see how this worked out with different age groups. You might just like to think where the chronically busy might stand . . .

But what about other people in very different contexts? How do they experience time? What are its qualities and characteristics? What about people who are in a conflict situation—who are living in a war zone? How do past, present and future stack up for them? And what of those living in the immediate aftermath of violence or trauma? Victims of Post-Traumatic Stress Disorder are locked into re-living their worst moments, and, like the person having a vivid nightmare, experience the negative feelings not as if they are real, but for real.

Eva Hoffman, who wrote a book simply called *Time*,

grew up in Poland after the war.[5] Introducing her book she suggests that, like the young Vladimir Nabokov, she is a bit of a "chronophobe" and so is both fascinated and frightened by the passing of time. For as long as she can remember she has always been aware of the ephemeral nature of time, whether it is the ticking of a clock in the night or the plod, plod of the walk home from school—there another second has passed into oblivion. This is the perspective which the inventor John Taylor built into his millennium clock at Corpus Christi College, Cambridge. Mounted above the time-telling device is a large grasshopper-like figure which opens and closes its mouth every second, eating time. Taylor calls it a "chronophage"—a time eater. The scary creature also winks knowingly at you from time to time, and the clock marks the hour not with a chime, but with the sound of a chain dropping into a coffin. The message is not only that time passes but that your time is passing away—every second gone is one less to live.

A thorough study of time could take a lifetime of intense activity and very few of us will be inclined to take that on. Yet one of the reasons that the new busy has such a stranglehold on so many of us is because we routinely fail to reflect on the nature of time and the way in which each of us is a temporal creature. So while not advocating that we get too much into the physics of time, I do suggest that we need to explore one or two of time's mysteries. A constricted understanding of time makes us vulnerable to the horrible trap of new busy.

[5] Eva Hoffman, *Time* (Profile Books, 2009).

PART 5

Two Types of Time

Perhaps the most important component of time wisdom is the appreciation that there are two types of time. The Greeks called them *chronos* and *kairos*. We can call them "clock time" and "opportunity time", but the Greek terms are shorter and you soon get used to them . . .

The problem with time management, and the reason it fuels the new busy, is that it focuses excessively on *chronos*, clock time.

There is good reason for doing so. Taylor's greedy and winking chronophage needs to be on our minds. There is no point thinking that we can have today again. What we don't get done today will need to be done tomorrow— assuming, that is, it really does need to be done.

What time management does is to focus on the demands of the chronophage. It is a battery of techniques, methods and attitudes to help us deal with the passing of time. It helps us to become more efficient and effective. It encourages us to take on board the lessons of the institutions in general and factories in particular and to find ways of doing things which take less time.

Time management is brilliant if your challenge is getting more done in less time. Used well, it will allow you to get your work finished in your work hours, have good weekends and holidays and enjoy a rich and rewarding retirement. If time were only *chronos*, clock time, then time management would be perfect. But it isn't, and that is why, without time wisdom, time management can go very wrong.

Time wisdom says that what matters about time is not only physics but biology, psychology and spirituality. People have complex needs, curious cycles and, thankfully, individual (and not always predictable) thoughts and feelings. This is why time is more than *chronos* for us. Time is also the opportunity, the wonder and mystery of the present moment. Time is a new turn of the kaleidoscope of possibilities which requires of us not efficient reaction, but creative response based on a careful reading of the ever changing patterns. This is part of the joy of life—but no time management tool can help you with it, because one of the great things about *kairos* is that it does not bow to *chronos*. On the contrary, it is *chronos* that must bow to *kairos*. "Stop all the clocks" was W.H. Auden's way of putting this (there is, by the way, much in the poetry of Auden to feed our time wisdom). The theologian Karl Barth put it in his own terms when he wrote that, "there is no god called *chronos*". What he meant was that while we might need to keep an eye on clock time, we are unwise to let it dominate us. To quote Auden again, "the clock on the mantelpiece / has nothing to recommend."

To understand that there are two types of time and that they make different claims on us is the beginning of time wisdom. The following table contrasts time management and time wisdom to give a richer sense of what mature and healthy time wisdom might look like. It first appeared in my book, *Beyond Busyness: Time Wisdom for Ministry*.[6]

TIME MANAGEMENT	TIME WISDOM
Focus on developing skills and habits.	Focus on developing wisdom and character.
Focus on *chronos* – ongoing time.	Equally concerned with issues of *kairos* (the moment of opportunity) and matters of timing more generally.
Applies particularly to the planning of tasks in relation to deadlines.	Applies to the realisation of high aspirations in complex environments.
Applies to the "work" environment.	Applies to the whole of life.
Based on the clock and calendar.	Based on the reality that the clock and calendar are only part of the story of "telling the time".
Focuses on doing more in less time—quantitative.	Focuses on doing the most important things as well as possible—qualitative.
Tends to involve convergent and analytical thought.	More open to imaginative and divergent thought.
Focus on self—what I can get done.	Focus on the wider community or team—how can we make the biggest difference.
Depends on strong boundaries and clear processes.	Sees boundaries and processes as a means to ends and so subject to transgression in the interests of higher aims.
Suspicious of multi-tasking.	Sees multi-tasking as normal.

---

[6] Stephen Cherry, *Beyond Busyness: Time Wisdom for Ministry* (Sacristy Press, 2012).

TIME MANAGEMENT	TIME WISDOM
Seeks to eliminate procrastination.	Emphasises the importance of getting the timing right, recognising that this will sometimes mean engaging in what looks like procrastination.
Sees time as limited, a scarce resource.	Sees time as both plentiful and relative.
Has no theology or spirituality of time.	Encourages a rich theology and spirituality of time and its stewardship.
Seeks to organise things so that the best use is made of the passing moments of present tense.	Is attentive to the demands and needs of the past, the future and the present.

**Figure 2: Table summarising the differences between
Time Management and Time Wisdom**

PART 6

Why Give Up Busyness?

Sir Edmund Hillary famously said that the reason for climbing Everest was simply "because it is there". The reason to give up busyness is simply because you can.

It seems impossible. The pressures are on and our lives often feel out of control. Whether the reason is that we have fallen into the Acceleration Trap—or work for an organisation that has fallen into it—or because we have somehow internalised the false message that new busy is good—that it makes our lives meaningful and us important—we *can* do something about it.

Before taking the plunge and trying to shake off the busyness thing, let's nail our colours to the mast and come clear. **Busyness is bad for you and bad for the people around you. It is fuelled not by purpose but by lack of purpose, not by courage but by anxiety, not by wisdom but by folly.** Edward Hallowell put it like this in his book *CrazyBusy*: "Being too busy is a persistent and pestering problem, one that is leading tens of millions of Americans to feel as if they were living in a swarm of gnats constantly taking bites out of their lives. All the screaming and swatting in the world does not make them go away."[7] (And as we know, it's not just Americans.)

---

[7] Edward M. Hallowell, *CrazyBusy: Overstretched, Overburdened and About to Snap!* (Ballantine Books, 2006).

Worse yet are the consequences. One of the ironies of busyness is that it deprives us of self-awareness. You probably don't know much about the way you behave when in the grip of new busy. However, you have probably been on the wrong end of someone else's busyness. If so—this is what you might have seen.

A chronically busy person is someone whose perception is distorted—who has become self-important and probably a bit grand. They have found a way of gaining admiration and sympathy from all around. But alas! This proves not to be satisfying and does not make them good company. In fact they are inclined to become rude and demanding—and of course impatient. At the same time the very busy person has a constant alibi for not getting things done. As we have already noted, he or she was simply too busy for *that*.

I have painted an ogre, perhaps, but do have some sympathy. Our ogre is in the grip of something—he or she is addicted to relentless action, stimulation, to the one-thing-after-another which is ultimately all *chronos* can deliver without *kairos* to add colour and depth to the moment. The busy-busy person is on the fast track to burnout and unhappiness—and yet their foot is on the accelerator.

Find that unattractive? It's time to press the brake.

STOP!

PART 7

What Does NOT BUSY Mean?

Well, it doesn't mean that you don't have anything to do or that you are free of demands, pressures or deadlines. It means that you are not in the grip of the busyness syndrome. When you are busy it is old busy you go through, something energising and in a modest way pleasurable. NOT BUSY means that life for you is more than doing things, that you have an eye on *kairos* as well as on *chronos*.

NOT BUSY does not mean that you will always be the first to arrive and last to leave, the sad one who is forever loitering. It does not mean that you will speak the most at a meeting because you have no concern about getting through the business in reasonable time. It does not mean that you are going to be negligent about obligations, duties or responsibilities because you are not bothered (NOT BOTHERED is a very different and entirely unworthy attitude). People who are NOT BUSY will not fail to attend to their own needs or to those of people around them. In fact they will be good, patient and loving carers; good partners, parents, and students. Being NOT BUSY does not mean I'm at a loose end. But it does mean that I'm ready to have my plans changed if a more important priority emerges. NOT BUSY requires both planning and flexibility. You do have to know what your aims and goals are, and you have to be clear about your priorities. You have to be able to say "no".

Why is the ability to say "no" so critical? Because only people who can say "no" have the right to be taken seriously when they say "yes".

There is well known Bible story which features three men—only one of whom was NOT BUSY. He is remembered to this day as the Good Samaritan.

The point about the Good Samaritan was that he was not too busy; he changed his plans. The Bible is full of people who were not too busy:

- Moses turned aside to see the burning bush. NOT BUSY.
- Abraham was hospitable to the three travellers who were angels. NOT BUSY.
- Jesus often withdrew to a quiet place to pray. NOT BUSY.
- Paul found ways of making his work fit around his ministry. NOT BUSY.

Thinking about our own lives, it is worth making a list about what they would be like if we were NOT BUSY.

People who are NOT BUSY:

- have time to stand and stare every day;
- keep an eye on the clock but are not ruled by it;
- say "yes" or "no" to requests or opportunities with equal confidence and sincerity;
- have time for people when they are needed;
- are prepared to change priorities in the light of

new evidence or changing circumstances.

Those are all positives. But there are some negative benefits too.

People who are NOT BUSY do not:

- Use "busy" as an excuse or as a power word;
- Do everything I hoped for;
- Ignore the needs of the present moment;
- See time as a scarce resource.

PART 8

Time is a Spiritual Issue

Time *is* a spiritual issue. That's one of the implications of the idea of *kairos*. It is a fundamental insight of Christianity. In fact it is common to all religions which uses a calendar to invite people to enter into different spiritual truths and mysteries at different times of the year. For many modern people, this feels like just the sort of top-down approach which undermines and squashes personal freedom and spiritual vitality. This is what sends people who have grown tired of religion off in pursuit of "spirituality". However, as all the great spiritual teachers and traditions insist, some kind of discipline and self-control is vital to spirituality.

Authentic spirituality does not deliver self-fulfilment or autonomy in the way modern people think of these things. True spirituality does not deliver more "me". True spirituality delivers a deeper connection with reality and ultimate purpose. It draws us out of ourselves and into relationship with God, other people and creation. And, since time is a fundamental dimension and aspect of creation, spirituality connects us more realistically with time. **Time wisdom is a form of practical, temporal, spirituality.** And spirituality always invites us to engage with time.

Buddhism, for instance, requires people to take time out of time in the form of meditation. Islam is hugely

concerned with time—knowing when best to pray, when Ramadan begins and ends. Rabbi Heschel calls Judaism a "*religion of time* aiming at *the sanctification of time*." He says that:

> Judaism teaches us to be attached to *holiness in time*, to be attached to sacred events, to learn how to consecrate sanctuaries that emerge from the magnificent stream of a year. The Sabbaths are our great cathedrals; and our Holy of Holies is a shrine that neither the Romans nor the Germans were able to burn; a shrine that even apostasy cannot easily obliterate: the Day of Atonement.[8]

Christianity is hugely invested in the question of time, using both the moon and the sun to help shape its calendar and itself giving structure and form to the secular calendar of the western world. It has not always found it easy to understand precisely how human beings, time and the sacred connect but one of Jesus' most memorable phrases is, "the Sabbath for man was made, not man for the Sabbath" (Mark 2.27). To modern ears the phrase, "time was made for people, not people for time" is perhaps closer to the challenge to cultural assumptions that Jesus was offering. This is a point that Paul seems to have absorbed, as he puts no pressure on the new churches to keep the Sabbath. And yet to suggest that Christian spirituality does not have its eye on the calendar, the clock and the moment is clearly absurd. There are few things that Christian people discuss more avidly or passionately than time. Not least if a sermon goes on a bit too long.

---

[8] Abraham Joshua Heschel, *The Sabbath* (Shambhala Publications, 1951), pp. xv–xvi (emphasis original)

If time is a spiritual issue, busyness is a sign than spirituality has grown old, tired and thin; that it is not able to bring nourishment and resource to where it is most needed—the very fast lane of the runaway world and its all too rapidly burning-out passengers. Busyness, in its new and chronic guise, is toxic to spirituality and to wellbeing precisely because it eliminates the possibility of the spiritual appreciation of the passing moment or special days as the cause of celebration. **Busyness commits us to a linear and superficial way of living which skates over reality as a skater skims over the surface of ice.** There is fun in this, but spirituality says that life is more like scuba-diving than skating. We are here to explore, inhabit and enjoy living. Not just to get things done or to rush from A to B.

To give up busyness, then, is to seek to walk through the door of the present moment into the world of spiritual delights and challenges. It is to take up the challenge of finding a spirituality which works for today—however busy today might be.

PART 9

How?

The pursuit of NOT BUSY is a lifetime's project, and most of us get there in the end, realising that it is precisely because time is running out that it is wise to take time and enjoy living.

It is never too late to start, but the I'M NOT BUSY campaign is based on the idea of giving up busyness right now.[9] Here are Ten Top Tips to help you with this significant spiritual challenge. Take a few minutes now to think through why they are good ideas and decide which of them might work best for you. Consider starting by choosing your top five and then narrowing them down to three.

- Decide never to describe yourself as busy.
- Don't let others get away with saying "I thought you'd be too busy".
- Take some time out to do nothing every day.
- Make a two-column "To Do" list regularly, with one column entitled "Must Do" and the other "May Do".
- Draw up a list of things you are not going to do (your "Don't Do" list).
- Stop using your smartphone as an alarm clock.
- Arrive and leave on time.
- Book your holiday well in advance.

---

[9] If you haven't seen it already, visit www.notbusy.co.uk.

- Earmark some time in your diary for "preparation" and some for "catch-up" every week.
- Tell someone else that you are giving up busyness and ask them to monitor you for "white rabbit behaviour".

Each of these is explained in the following chapter.

PART 10

Tips on Implementing the Ten Top Tips

1. Decide never to describe yourself as busy.

In fact, it would probably be better to stop using the word altogether as it rarely does any good—unless preceded by the word "not". It has become a cliché to be busy and clichés often stop people being imaginative, bright and positive.

If this feels difficult, think about words you might use instead. There are two sorts: those which more accurately describe "old busy" and those which describe the "new busy". Words like "hectic" or "frantic" are examples of the good type of busy. "Today has been a bit frantic." "This week was hectic." This puts a limit on your out-of-control-ness and points to a normal way of life which is not busy.

As for words which describe the new busy—these are more difficult to utter.

Examples include:

"Actually my life is out of control."

"I am panicking because I am trying to do lots of things

that are desirable but not necessary."

"I am neglecting my children" (or parents—depending on your age, and theirs).

These are the sorts of things that new busy actually means—and if we heard them come out of our own mouths we would be ashamed and stop.

2. Don't let others get away with saying "I thought you'd be too busy".

On hearing about the I'M NOT BUSY campaign, one person immediately sent a tweet about this tip: "Yes, they do and it really bugs me." Being bugged by this is two thirds of the battle. Most people simply collude with it; I know, I get it all the time. It does, I confess, make me feel quite good. The person who is speaking to me has recognised the pressure I am under. That's nice.

Except that it isn't really nice and it isn't necessarily true. There are loads of reasons why we might say to someone's face we expect that they are busy. One is that we can see how frazzled they are and we are recognising this by putting our own agenda for interaction with them in second place. Another is that this is code for a bit of deference: by saying that "you *are* busy" we are implying that "I am less busy" and giving them busy-status, recognising their importance. But you can easily imagine the possibility of someone asking how you are, saying they expect that you are very busy and using your agreement with that to introduce a sympathy session for you *which you don't want*. This is manipulative, but like all manipulation the manipulated is vulnerable because the manipulator has seen a weakness of which they, the manipulated, are not self-aware.

How can this be addressed? Here are some possibilities:

Gambit: **I expect you are very busy.**
Response: Actually I try not to use the word.

Gambit: **I expect you are very busy.**
Response: There's always plenty to do, but I enjoy most of it so that's fine.

Gambit: **I expect you are very busy.**
Response: Well, this week (or today) has been a bit hectic, but next week (or tomorrow) will be okay.

Gambit: **I expect you are very busy.**
Response: Never too busy to talk to you. Shall we have five minutes now?

Gambit: **I expect you are very busy.**
Response: I am today. But let's make a time to meet soon. Email me.

Gambit: **I expect you are very busy.**
Response: Only because I am planning my summer
            holiday/next weekend away/day off/trip to
            the cinema.

Gambit: **I expect you are very busy.**
Response: I used to be. But I gave it up.

3. Take some time out to do nothing every day.

This is where you can make some real progress by using
time management ideas and techniques wisely. But first,
you have to *want* to do it.

Second, you have to decide where and when to do it.
Making it the same time and same place every day is very
helpful if your life has some sort of shape and routine.
That way you will soon be able to harness the power of
habit to keep you on the straight and narrow. The problem
with relying on that is that when things change and our
routine goes to pot so too does this particular discipline.
It is probably best just to note that for now and go for
the building up a habit approach.

Third, as well as setting a time and place you need to
decide "how long". Most phones have a timer on them,
and this is one of the ways your phone can be your ally
against busyness. My suggestion is that you start with ten
minutes. It doesn't sound like much but can feel like an
eternity. Then every week increase it by one minute until

you get up to what feels like the right amount of time for you. If trying ten minutes drives you to distraction—don't give up, start with five.

Fourth, you must do nothing. This doesn't mean read the paper or listen to music, walk, run or travel by bus, car or train or plane (though you can also use travel times for this kind of busy-busting exercise). If you are in a place where noise can distract you then some ambient music through headphones can help—but you don't need tunes or polyphony, never mind romantic symphonies or intellectual quartets. The point is not to be entertained or stimulated, but to settle into the pulse of time.

Fifth, to be frank we are talking about meditation here. So any meditation guide will help. The basics are: sit in a formal, not sloppy, pose: feet on the floor, hands still, back upright but comfortably supported. Breathe deeply—from below the diaphragm—put your hand on your tummy to feel it move in and out. Pay attention to your breathing. Let it show. Match the in and out with a mantra—a few words which you can repeat over and over. Words and phrases from the scriptures can be excellent for this, and help ground you in a timeless tradition. Don't get agitated by your attention wandering but let it keep coming back to your breathing, your mantra, the passing of time. This is time for time and it will impact on the way in which you inhabit time all day. Once you get into this you will probably benefit from finding a spiritual guide.

4. Make a two-column "To Do" list regularly.

For me this is one of the most powerful antidotes to the busyness syndrome. I never really got on with the standard time management idea of making a "To Do" list every day. It was probably mostly laziness and list-allergy, but there was more to it than that. When I did get round to doing it, there were so very many things I wanted to put on it that the whole thing was overwhelming.

The two-column list is another matter. It does involve a bit of extra work on your behalf before you start, but it's not as taxing as you might think. You just have to put a vertical line down the middle of the page. To the left of the line you list the things you really *must* do today. To the right you list the things that you'd like to do, that you *may* do.

This is like the job description which distinguishes between essential and desirable attributes of the applicants. It's a really simple distinction but makes all the difference—especially to people who have quite a lot of discretion about what they do. Such people include very senior people in corporations, self-employed people, carers and others who work at home or from home, leaders in any sector, public, private or voluntary, people in pastoral ministry, academics, teachers and students. And these are just the sort of people who are prone to suffer from busyness syndrome because there is no rigid structure or tough line-manager to organise their day.

5. Draw up a list of things you are not going to do (your "Don't Do" list).

Now we are talking. This is the heart of the matter. The "To Don't" or "Don't Do" list is the most liberating but also the most demanding tool of all. You will probably need some help to get your list drawn up—and some serious support to enable you actually *not* to do the things that are on it.

One way of doing this is to have it as a follow-on task from the two–column list. When you have made it up you simply cross things off the list. The logical thing to do is to remove desirables but human beings are not entirely logical and so that will probably not work. You need to keep some desirables—some *merely* desirables—in there. These are your motivators, the things you really like doing even if they are not strictly speaking necessary. Life will get better if you can strike off some of those "must do" items. But how are you going to do that?

Well, here is a principle that might help you start. "There is always someone to talk to". It may not be obvious who it is, but someone is there—a friend, family member, colleague, boss, junior, counsellor, trainer, therapist, minister or coach who can help. Maybe it is the person sitting opposite you on the train. Someone not far away from you might just give you support you need to address this question: "There is something I have to do which feels like a really important duty but for one reason or another it seems to be there just clogging up my diary and making my life too busy. How do you feel about giving me five minutes to work out whether I should get rid of it or not?" I don't know this for sure, of course, but my guess is that 90% of the people you ask would love it that you have asked their advice. Why not go for it? You are not giving away personal responsibility but seeking support in exercising it wisely.

To draw up a "Don't Do" list will always require a bit of courage. You can't do it without disappointing someone. Very often the person you will have to disappoint is yourself. You would love to do it all and meet everyone's expectations but—here comes some time wisdom—"you can't".

So, to develop a good "Don't Do" list you have to first bite the bullet of self-awareness which says that you can't do everything.

There is another approach to the "Don't Do" list which is even more time wise. When you recognise that things are not right, when you sense that your busyness has got out of hand, when you look at your diary and feel your heart sinking . . . On these occasions it is not enough just to score a few things out at random—or to report to the GP with stress (that is to act too late and won't of itself solve the problem. It just gives you some time to recover. That may be just what you need, but when you have recovered you need to take action).

Rather, the day you reach this kind of crisis point is just the moment to launch your own personal "don't do it" project. If you are busy the last thing that you feel you need is another project. But believe me you need this one. This is the project which says, "the last twelve months have been dreadful but the next twelve months are going to be liveable". It is the project which says, "I give myself six weeks, two months, three months"—however long, you decide—"to make my life less busy".

Once you have declared the project "on", your task is to do the necessary behind the scenes work to reduce the number of time-consuming things that you are committed to. Again it will probably be as well to tell someone else what you are trying to do and get their support, encouragement and companionship on the journey. You will definitely meet resistance because you have been busy making yourself indispensable for the last however long. But the corner has to be turned and at some key point in the project—say a fortnight in—you will have come up with a list of things you are *not* going to do anymore. That list is your passport to a richer, calmer, more creative life, and a far more pleasant time for your family and friends.

6. Stop using your smartphone as an alarm clock.

Writing in *The Guardian*'s "Weekend" section on Saturday 26th January 2013, Arianna Huffington, founder of the Huffington Post, wrote about the value of sleep. She has become, she writes, a "sleep evangelist" and sent many of her friends an old fashioned alarm clock to save them having their smartphone by their bed.

I was delighted to read the article. I had fallen for that one in the past. Seduced by the amazing capacities of the BlackBerry I wanted it to do as much as it possibly could for me. Its range of alarm tunes was fun to explore and I found a nice sound to wake up to. The snag, of course, were those wretched little stars that appear on the screen to tell you that you have a text or email waiting to be read. Or the red flashing light that lets you know that you have been mentioned in a tweet. That perfectly designed red star is pretty difficult to resist at the best of times. But when your defences are down and you are half asleep, it finds it easier to get the edge over you. You are curious, you look, you read, and suddenly the most precious time of your day has been invaded by demands and stresses that should be quite alien to it.

Maybe you are stronger willed than I am (I certainly hope that you are!). Either way, why let temptation into the room? Get a clunky old alarm clock, or a snazzy digital one, and set it for a reasonable, sustainable hour. As Huffington says in the same article, people can get very macho about how little sleep they take. Confronted at a dinner party by someone boasting that he only had four hours the night before, she says that she "resisted the temptation to tell him that dinner might have been a lot more interesting if he'd had five". The point made me chuckle, but notice that she didn't actually make the comment to him. People rarely do when we are boring, boorish or just a pain in the neck. We have to work it out for ourselves.

7. **Arrive and leave on time.**

The counselling profession is great at time management. You get a 50 minute appointment and that's it. Clients and patients may find this a bit tough to start with but they get used to it and before long are raising the issues that need half an hour, half an hour before for the end. It's the same with anyone and any group. Just as work expands to fill the time available, conversations, discussion and consultations can be fitted into the amount of time they deserve (rather than the amount of time that they want or would all too easily sprawl into). The key is to budget the time and to be prompt in starting and precise in finishing.

Now there are occasions on which a time-wise person will break this rule—whereas a mere time manager will never do so. But while flexibility is wisdom, lack of structure and discipline is folly.

Start on time. Begin on time; not early, but on time. Get things wound up in the agreed time frame—whether it is formal or informal. And be prepared to ask the question—when will this end? How long should I allocate for this meeting? If no one has thought about it then maybe they should. Very few meetings need to go on for "as long as it takes". Yes, that might sometimes be the case in a crisis, but the basis of this campaign against the new busy is that while a crisis is a crisis, normal life is lived at a sustainable pace.

A wise human being will know that they cannot control many things—and they will not want to. Controlling consumes enormous amounts of energy and the desire to control is always spotted by others and resented. But you *can* control yourself. If it's time to go—go. You don't need to make the chair end the meeting. Use what people sometimes call the "law of two feet". Stand up and move. If you do it three minutes before you absolutely really must move then so much the better, it means you have time for a two-minute chat with someone en route.

8. Book your holiday well in advance.

On 30th December 2012 I posted a list of nine New Year's resolutions for busy people on my blog.[10] The list overlaps with this list of ten tips but one of them was more specific, "get all your holiday booked in by the end of January". Towards the end of the month I got a tweet from someone saying that they had done exactly that and was delighted. They would not have done so had I not nudged them via the blog.

It's not very difficult to appreciate why it is important and valuable to plan and prepare our time off, but, as I mentioned in the blog, people have made a study of this and found that "Predictable Time Off" is more enjoyable and better for you than random time off. Having said that, a bit of random time off can have its own delights. But not knowing when your holiday is going to be can in itself be a stress which aggravates the feeling of busyness.

---

[10] http://stephencherry.wordpress.com/2012/12/30/
nine-new-years-resolutions-for-busy-people/

Think about it: how can you plan a good vacation, take the best advantage of offers, and enjoy the excitement of looking forward to it if you don't know when it's going to be?

So this one is neither rocket science nor especially difficult. But if you find that you haven't got time to get the holiday into your diary you really are suffering from busyness and need to head for suggestions 3 or 4 above as a place to start.

9. Earmark some time in your diary for "preparation" and some for "catch-up" every week.

I can't believe how obvious this idea is—and yet it was only recently that I decided to put in some unallocated "preparation" time into my diary each week. The reason? I suddenly found myself with no time to prepare for things I had never done before. It was a bit scary.

We all wing it a bit. We have to busk from time to time; improvisation is absolutely part of life, and a very good part of life. Being creative on the hoof is energising and exciting. I am also very clear that it is impossible to prepare for every eventuality, but when winging it becomes normal you are on your way to becoming boring, predictable and repetitive. And repetitive. Yes, repetitive. Very repetitive.

As for "catch-up", that matters too and more than we think. Whether it is just filing papers away—in the filing cabinet or in the round thing that sits on the floor—working through the action points, writing up the minutes or the *aide-memoire* of a meeting, or writing thank you letters or booking the venue for the same time next year. Follow-up often matters as much as the meeting. If it is not done quickly and effortlessly the need for it fuels that nagging sense that things are out of control which lies behind busyness.

So you need to two sessions in the diary each week which are kept free of meetings and appointments: one for preparation, one for follow-up. If they can be the same time each week that will build a rhythm that will help you when the going gets tough, but it is much, much better to have them in there somewhere rather than not at all.

If you don't have space in your diary to schedule in preparation and follow-up then maybe you really do need to get straight stuck into a major "don't-do-it" project because it seems that busyness has you by the throat.

10. Tell someone else that you are giving up busyness and ask them to monitor you for "white rabbit behaviour".

In my book *Beyond Busyness: Time Wisdom for Ministry*[11] I suggest that when people are busy being busy they behave like the White Rabbit in *Alice in Wonderland*.

---

[11] Stephen Cherry, *Beyond Busyness: Time Wisdom for Ministry* (Sacristy Press, 2012).

They have quick, jerky movements, they speak in short sentences, they think in bullet points, their eyes dart about and they exude self-importance. They pay no attention to their peripheral vision and tend not to listen—indeed seem to have lost the listening function. Busy people rush off looking at their watches while muttering, "I'm late, I'm late".

We all do this stuff, or most of us anyway, some of the time. But we tend not to be aware of it; hence the idea of deliberately giving up busyness. This suggestion is a simple and obvious one, based on the same principle as several of the others, that it is not only good to have an intention and make an effort, but also to enlist people who are close to you as your critical friends as you try to make some progress.

Again, people are almost certainly more willing to help than you are to ask for help. So go for it, make it be known that you are trying to give up busyness and ask people to tell you when you start to resemble the White Rabbit.

You can make this fun of course—get people to mime a rabbit face at you as a code, or to email you, "White Rabbit Behaviour! Tuesday 2.45" or to tweet #WRB to you. Feedback like this really can work—and takes more or less no time at all unless you get defensive.

P.S. Don't get defensive. It is very time-consuming.

PART 11
A Non-Busy Life

We have looked at the problem, examined its intricacies and found some ways to address it, but what does a non-busy life look like?

It's worth having an answer to this somewhere in your mind for two reasons. First, so that you know what you are aiming at. Second, because you can actually cheat a bit at this. Don't worry, it is not bad cheating—it is good and wise cheating based on sound psychological principles.

This is how it works. We know that human minds are very significantly influenced by their bodies. There is a kind of positive feedback which makes you think that your true internal state is a reflection of your external or bodily state. For instance, experiments have shown that if you hold a pencil cross-ways between your teeth (so that you smile) you will find a cartoon funnier than if you hold the same pencil lengthwise so that you purse your lips.[12]

What this means is that if you go about being frantically and chronically busy, you will end up feeling busy and telling everyone, verbally or non-verbally, that you really are very busy. Busyness feeds on itself which is why it can quickly snowball to toxic levels in individuals, groups

---

[12] See Daniel Kahneman, *Thinking, Fast and Slow* (Allen Lane, 2011), p. 54.

and institutions. Busyness is not only a disease—it is infectious.

Once you know about this positive feedback mechanism you can use it to help fight the good fight against busyness. All you need to do is to identify some NOT BUSY behaviours and start to practice them. Very soon this will impact on your attitude and outlook and these same behaviours will become the new new normal for you—a post-busy or beyond busyness normal which is what this guide to giving up busyness has had as its sole aim all along.

So, here are some examples of not-busy behaviours. Keep them in mind as you aim to adopt them as your practice as you give up busyness for good.

- Walk calmly, positively and purposefully.
- Ignore anything marked "URGENT".
- Never sigh on arrival or say "phew".
- Say to yourself, "no one is indispensable—not even me".
- Never tell people what you are about to do next or "rush on to".
- Never say, "this evening I have three meetings to attend all at the same time".
- Don't tell people that you have missed your day off.
- Do tell people what you do when you have some free time.

PART 12

It's Micro-Party Time!

One of the unfortunate consequences of getting very busy is that you get lost in your own tail-spin. You become more of an individual, but not in the good sense of a richer personality. On the contrary, busyness leads to loneliness and it is no surprise that today's busyness epidemic goes along with a rise in social isolation and the breakdown of community. In terms of a phrase made famous by Robert Putnam: people who "bowl alone" do so partly because they don't have time to join a group or a team. Or, to use an old fashioned word, they don't have time to make up a party.

At several points in this all-too-hasty introduction to time wisdom, the suggestion has been to engage with other people, whether to ask their wisdom or to get them to give you some feedback. That's important, both to help you learn and also because interactions really do help slow you down a bit. Social life has its pace. Every community has its pulse.

Have you ever noticed that meetings seem to take a long time? It's all to do with the pace of the social. A time wise chair or facilitator will recognise this and work with the grain of it, not giving in to the slowest person in the room but finding a way of making the pace appropriate. This should involve both slowing down and speeding up. Either can be wise in different circumstances. Plodding on can sap energy and purpose and yet to do everything as fast as possible, on the other hand, burns people up and isolates them from each other.

This leads on to the final aspect of time wisdom in this crash course, which is the suggestion that you make some party time each day. This is not to advocate hours and hours of self-indulgence. The suggestion is rather that **there is scope several times a day for a bit of a micro-party**.

Meal times used to be like this, as did coffee and tea breaks. Today meals and drinks are often taken in front of a screen: computer if you are working, TV if you are not.

Yes! I am advocating that you listen to others and talk about the everyday things of life. These are the practices of a healthy and spiritual person. The heart and art of this is to talk about the things that impinge but which we can't even imagine controlling. Once you begin to talk about something you *can* do something about, the nature of your conversation changes and you start living in the future. That's why the weather (apologies to any non-British readers) is a truly brilliant topic of conversation. Always changing, it is never my responsibility.

Be on the lookout for micro-parties, interactions which take just a moment or two. We are taught as children that strangers are a danger to us, but most strangers hold no threat to adults. Let other people slow you down, even if just a tiny bit. It won't destroy your day. That's the trouble with a time management approach which insists on eliminating all "wasted time". If you pursue it to its logical conclusion, it removes one of the main protections that we have against the runaway life towards which the new busy propels us: the mini-breaks and the micro-parties which punctuate life lived at a human pace.

PART 13

Finally . . .

Now that you are getting into living life neither in the slow nor the fast lane, but in a sensibly yet variably paced middle lane—the lane which feels human and in which the spirituality of time begins to be part of your awareness—do spare a thought for everyone else. See them speeding past. Be aware of them as they crash out, not to enjoy the view or see the sunrise or to watch the clouds float or birds soar, but to recover just-enough energy, or drink just-enough coffee, to be able to drive on again.

You have invested an hour—maybe a bit less, maybe a bit more—reading this book. How can you get others to steer themselves away from the acceleration trap?

Certainly enlisting them as your White Rabbit behaviour monitor is a good start. Follow that up by drawing their attention to the "I'M NOT BUSY" campaign, through the website (www.notbusy.co.uk) or Facebook page. Retweeting anything from @TimeWisdom will pass on some tiny time-wise gem to all of your followers.

The most influential thing of all is your own behaviour and the attitudes that it reveals. If you seriously do believe that there is *not* enough time for a human being to enjoy living, then you are in trouble. If deep down you trust that actually a life well lived is one which has time and which makes time for others, which appreciates that good things mature slowly and is not that is not always seeking to control . . . then you are more than half way there. You just need to find the wisdom, strength, courage and company that will help you put your foot on the brake, slow down and start to live again.

Go for it.

Say: "I'M NOT BUSY".

Printed by BoD°in Norderstedt, Germany

9 781908 381132